MACHINES

AIRPLANES

by Wendy Strobel Dieker

AMICUS | AMICUS INK

cockpit

wing

Look for these words and pictures as you read.

jets

control stick

Look! There goes an airplane!
How does it fly?

cockpit

See the cockpit?
There is the pilot.
He flies the plane.

The plane needs a fast start.
It speeds down the runway.
Up it goes!

wing

See the wing?
Two wings help lift the plane.
Up, up and away!

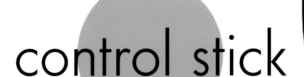

control stick

See the control stick?

The pilot turns it.

It steers the plane.

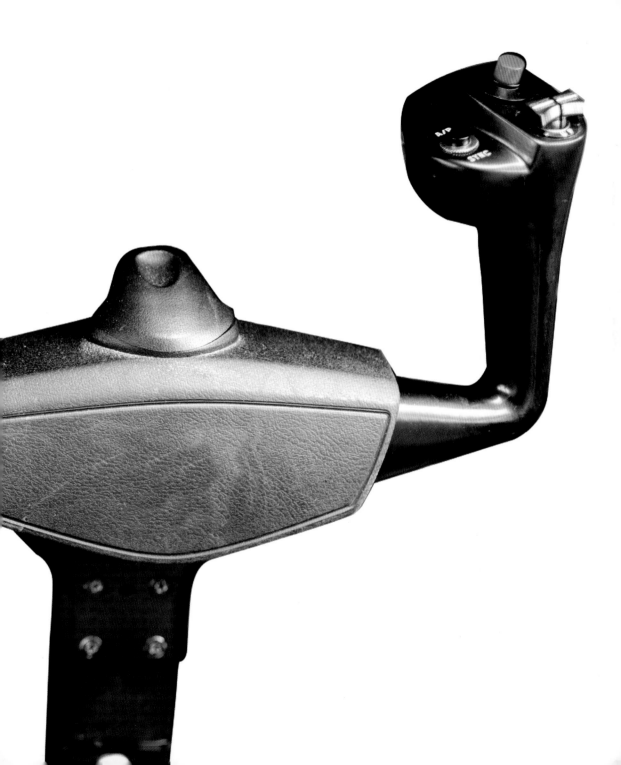

jets

See the jets?
They make the plane
go fast. Zoom!

Airplanes fly people to far away places!

cockpit

wing

Did you find?

jets

control stick

Spot is published by Amicus and Amicus Ink
P.O. Box 1329, Mankato, MN 56002
www.amicuspublishing.us

Library of Congress Cataloging-in-Publication Data
Names: Dieker, Wendy Strobel, author.
Title: Airplanes / by Wendy Strobel Dieker.
Description: Mankato, Minnesota : Amicus, [2020] | Series:
 Spot. Mighty machines | Audience: K to grade 3.
Identifiers: LCCN 2018024619 (print) | LCCN
 2018036466 (ebook) | ISBN 9781681517261 (pdf)
 | ISBN 9781681516448 (library binding) | ISBN
 9781681524306(pbk.)
Subjects: LCSH: Airplanes--Juvenile literature. | Airplanes-
 -Parts--Juvenile literature. | CYAC: Airplanes. | LCGFT:
 Instructional and educational works. | Picture books.
Classification: LCC TL547 (ebook) | LCC TL547 .D544 2020
 (print) | DDC 629.133/34--dc23
LC record available at https://lccn.loc.gov/2018024619

Printed in China

HC 10 9 8 7 6 5 4 3 2 1
PB 10 9 8 7 6 5 4 3 2 1

Alissa Thielges, editor
Deb Miner, series designer
Aubrey Harper, book designer
Holly Young, photo researcher

Photos by Shutterstock/Rob Wilson
cover; iStock/ideeone cover; Alamy/
Cristian M. Vela 1, 16; Alamy/Eugene
Feygin 3; Shutterstock/Kiwis 4-5;
Alamy/Allen Creative/Steve Allen
6-7; iStock/guvendemir 8-9; iStock/
Elenathewise 10-11; iStock/EXTREME-
PHOTOGRAPHER 12-13; Shutterstock/
alredosaz 14-15

AIRPLANES

9